JOURNAL

PETER PAUPER PRESS, INC.
WHITE PLAINS, NEW YORK

Copyright © 2008
Peter Pauper Press, Inc.
202 Mamaroneck Avenue
White Plains, NY 10601
All rights reserved
ISBN 978-1-59359-490-9
Printed in China
7

Visit us at www.peterpauper.com

Critical Care & High Acuity Nursing Care Notes

Components of Blood:
   - Formed Elements (cells) = 45% →
leukocytes (WBC), Erythrocytes (RBC) = Hemoglobin
which transports O2, thrombocytes = Blood Clotting Plate
   - Plasma = 55% → Proteins (Albumin →
osmotic Pressure of blood), (Globulins → Antibodies),
(Fibrinogen → Blood clotting), Water, other =
cell metabolism.

* Note: Adult Body holds average of 5L. of blood

Formation of Blood Cells:
   - Cell differentiation = maturation Process
a blood cell undergoes.
   - Undifferentiated has no specific functions yet
   - A fully differentiated Blood Cell has 2
major characteristics: It only has 1 function
   + it Can No longer Reproduce.

* Note: chronic hypoxia induces Secretion of
Erythropoietin that ↑ production of RBC's.

Organs & Tissue of the Immune System:
   Primary Lymph organs = Bone Marrow & thymus
which are major cytes of Lympocyte develop=ment.
   -Secondary Lymph Organs = Tonsils & adenoids,
Lymph nodes, Spleen . * Celluelar & humcral
Responses occur in the Secondary Lymphoid
organs. *
   -Spleen Responds to Primary blood bourne
antigens
   - Lymph nodes respond to antigens Circulating
in Lymph System

The Spleen : Serves 3 funtions.
   - 1st = Site for the distruction of injured &
wornaut RBC's.
   - 2nd = is a Reservoir for B-cells
   - 3rd = Serves as a Storage Site for Blood,
   which is Released from distended vessels
   in times of demand.

Components of Oxygen Transport : Erythrocytes
 - RBC's are far more Plentiful of the blood
 cells
 - RBC's are measured in (mcl)
 - They Live fairly long → 120 days.

Erythropoiesis : RBC's = O_2 transport via
 hemoglobin ; & regulation is based on
 level of tissue Oxygenation .
 - RBC's Arise from Red Bone marrow,
 they mature in the Spleen
 - Tightly regulated by erythropoietin
 which is a hormone produced by Kidney
 - The minerals Iron & Copper are important
 for hemoglobin Synthesis & Strong Plasma
 membranes.   *Erythrocyte
        ↑ RBC   Production   ↓.
   ↓ tissue ↗ Production   ↑ tissue
   ↓ O_2 O_2

        ↑   . Disorders .
        | interfer w/ tissue ←
        | O_2
        |_____   - Anemia
                          - Hypotension
                          - Hypovolemia
                          - Pulmonary diseases

Hemoglobing (H6b):